Volume 108 of the Yale Series of Younger Poets

# ERUV

*Eryn Green*

*Foreword by Carl Phillips*

Yale UNIVERSITY PRESS/NEW HAVEN & LONDON

Published with assistance from a grant to honor James Merrill.
Published with assistance from the Mary Cady Tew Memorial Fund.

Yale University Press books may be purchased in quantity for educational, business,
or promotional use. For information, please e-mail sales.press@yale.edu (U.S.
office) or sales@yaleup.co.uk (U.K. office).

Designed by Mary Valencia
Set in Mrs. Eaves type by Integrated Publishing Solutions
Printed in the United States of America.

*Library of Congress Cataloging-in-Publication Data*
Green, Eryn, 1984–
    [Poems. Selections]
    Eruv / Eryn Green ; foreword by Carl Phillips. — First edition.
        pages cm. — (Yale series of younger poets ; vol. 108)
    ISBN 978-0-300-20125-3 (hardback) — ISBN 978-0-300-20122-2
(paperback)
    I. Title
    PS3607.R43275A6    2014
    811'.6—dc23                                        2013036825

A catalogue record for this book is available from the British Library.

This paper meets the requirements of ANSI/NISO Z39.48-1992
(Permanence of Paper).

10   9   8   7   6   5   4   3   2   1

*For Don who taught me to see,*
*Tome who taught me to read,*
*and my family who loved me*

They seemed glad to get out of themselves, and as if unwilling to be brought in. I was sometimes tempted to stretch an awning over them and take my seat there. It was worth the while to see the sun shine on these things, and hear the free wind blow on them; so much more interesting most familiar objects look out of doors than in the house.

—H. D. Thoreau

But pretty much where you get lost is in the forest.

—Jack Spicer

# CONTENTS

3

Notational, highly fragmented, wildly associative, as at ease apparently with seeming non sequitur as with the occasional sly literary allusion (Frederick Douglass, John Ashbery, Robin Blaser among them), the poems of Eryn Green's *Eruv* may eschew an easy discursiveness, but together they find their own way toward delivering an ultimately hopeful meditation on, if not paradise exactly, then the paradisiacal—the possibilities for it, the capacity in each of us to in fact create it.

> I was happy, paradise
>
> was a physical thing

says Green in "Thanksgiving," and indeed *Eruv* opens, with "First Walk," on a landscape that seems largely untouched by humanity, a space of light and vegetation that possesses its own particular kind of motion, unsteadying, teeming, dispersed, emptying, discharging. Not until the fifth part of this six-part poem do we encounter an I, who then as quickly disappears. Shortly after, there are "jets passing," there's a "voice saying // *not mine*," reminding us of a "far-off voice" that appeared earlier, though assigned to no one. We stand at the intersection of the paradisiacal and a decidedly disembodied human presence—as if paradise were the dominant force, overwhelming the human? Or as if our attempts to make inroads to paradise can only *be* attempts, and partial ones at that?

Twice in *Eruv*, the phrase "To be the mast of such great admiral" appears—a variation on "to be the mast of some great Ammiral," lines 292–93 of Milton's *Paradise Lost,* where Satan's spear is being described. To what effect, this allusion? I think this may be Green's way of obliquely pointing to the lostness of a paradise that the sensibility informing these poems clearly longs for. And yet, as the opening to *Eruv* suggests, paradise isn't so much lost, perhaps, as hard to access. Even the form of "First Walk" suggests something at once of separate spaces and an implied impulse, on the part of the text, to cross borders:

Far edge of October and still no frost—   converging wind patterns
                              reflecting across      pond-reflected lilies
                   small clearing. Unsteadying

..................................................................................................

of goldenrod

yellow light elbowing across

tall bushes

far-off voice

In other moments, instead of text, there's "merely" white space for a place to cross to:

Afternoon opening into vacant lot—   just a few thin sticks
          surrounded by gold-tipped weeds      and a small silver rainbird
streams across the scene—

                   all light sources   *teeming*
..................................................................................................

In both instances, though, the form seems an enactment of the book's concerns, our desire for another, better space, and the frustration of that desire. Here's where an eruv—or its equivalent—can prove useful. Green defines an eruv as "a ritual enclosure that opens private into public spaces"—allows passage, that is, between such spaces. For Green, the required eruv would seem to be nothing less than love—both as temporary passageway to paradise and as sometime distraction from paradise's lostness to us:

> suddenly my life
>
> makes sense: I get along
>
> until the cloud just collapses—
>
> I am standing on the freeway
>
> and cars move by like drunk panthers
>
> I am loved again
>
> like there was future again—
>
> ["Sounds (Second Walk)"]

Other times, the beloved is a door that exits out of lostness itself:

> don't know what to do with
> myself having never felt more
> lost and found you
> and a door
>
> ["Midnight Suns"]

"[T]he future is / love or isn't future at all" ("Anglers [So Soon]"). "[H]ow we survive / our own sleep is a question / but not tenderness" ("As the Sky Contained My Garden, I Opened My Door"). Clearly, love is the answer. But surely love is no less difficult to gain access to—and hold on to—than paradise, given "all the jackals of the heart," given "*I'm sorry I love you,*" and given the notion of need and how "we wrap ourselves up against" need and lack:

Hulking
the way it comes at me
two quivering palms full
of pine needle, the need
you say they signify, the lack
the way we wrap ourselves up against—

["Anglers (So Soon)"]

Isn't love at least a form of need?

Part of the conundrum of being human is that it means containing those elements that both set our desires in motion and have the ability to derail any satisfaction of those desires—restlessness is part of the problem, but so is our human need to rationalize:

Because as soon as we can read
our own nakedness, eden is foreign
to us—exegesis always already
baggage, the question of how
how we see changes
everything, oranges
for instance, the inscrutable meaning
of *this* Mardi Gras—

["Hymnal Oranges"]

If an instinct—an appetite—for exegesis (which can include the particular search for meaning that poetry is) makes us human, are we doomed from the start, caught in a longing for a love—for a paradise—that we estrange *ourselves* from?

That's one way to see it, yes. Another approach, suggested by the poems in the final movement of *Eruv,* is a kind of acceptance of our human complicatedness ("I like people/which makes for difficulties" ["Available"]), a willingness to rally in the face of brokenness but perhaps a healthy respect for brokenness, as well ("ok/I give in. All undone" ["Available"]). This way of thinking may not resolve our dilemma, but it allows us to be a little more at peace with it, maybe—we've moved from one space, psychologically, to another, from

the trees again

again saying *don't devolve*

*into a lesser you*

don't be base—
["The Disaster Takes Care of Everything"]

to

A world
in which I have made mistakes
and we are still perfect—

["Last Pier"]

and from the earlier impulse toward exegesis to

I had ideas about water once
they were the first
to wash away
with the rain.

["Bon Vivant"]

Perhaps the mind itself, then—imagination—as an eruv? Or more particularly, Keats's negative capability as eruv, and an ability to trust that from apparent dissolution a kind of wholeness can emerge, as at the end of "Dear Beings I Can Feel Your Hands":

world where

gates ajar        rend my prayer

where

> *wren—*

The poem seems quite literally to come undone, and yet I find here a meaningful anagrammatic kind of wordplay, in which the letters of "rend" (a tearing apart) and "where" (fixed location) give birth to "*wren,*" an image of physical wholeness capable of flight, one place to another.

> I start looking
> forward to an open door
> the thing that happens
> next—the world
> opens up

["Radio Silence"]

or, as Green puts it at the end of "Sedes," "We go over the cliffs at last" (paralleling, not so incidentally, the "*enormous brown leaves /* going over the falls" in *Eruv*'s opening poem, as if at last we'd become one, or almost, with that elusive paradise). And then what? Green seems to have learned to abandon this question, to exist instead in that liminal space between past and future, i.e., the present, the laughter and flowers with which *Eruv* closes as "shining / evidence, event of this" ("Rings").

*Eruv* is a book that surprised me first by its risks—the risk of, frankly, odd language (or the odd deployment of it), the risk of engaging seriously with beauty, that of the natural world especially; and the risk of addressing such abstractions as love and sorrow, triumph and fear, not with irony or detachment but with a confident authority. I've a sense that these poems not only had to be written, but written in exactly this way. *Eruv* is a brave debut, one that gives us the depth and complexity of the human condition—challenging, to say the least, overwhelming often, and yet, in the hands of this poet, shot through in the end with a heady, restorative joy.

—*Carl Phillips*

ERUV

On the Sabbath, carrying objects or bodies from one domain to another is prohibited by the Torah. An eruv (Hebrew: *mixture*) is a ritual enclosure that opens private into public spaces, fashioning a larger home out of shared alleys and courtyards, enabling transport between worlds. An eruv is best understood as a doorway; without one, carrying keys or tissues or pushing carriages would not be possible.

I

First Walk

Far edge of October and still no frost—      converging wind patterns
                 reflecting across        pond-reflected lilies
            small clearing. Unsteadying

..........................................................................................

            of goldenrod

         yellow light elbowing across

           tall bushes

               far-off voice

Afternoon opening into vacant lot—    just a few thin sticks

        surrounded by gold-tipped weeds     and a small silver rainbird

streams across the scene—

        all light sources     *teeming*

..................................................................................................................

Bright copper  seed husks

        organizing the field hush—

bright swaths of prairie flax catalyzed into shaking  *dispersed by some*  quick
                                        shift of thistle

   outside fissure of rocks made visible
...............................................................................................

        *Here/then*      ribbons past—

Gate-eyed in the clearing, I stand up and the whole thing's
invited—already summoning

struck beneath the greening

born again and again and all the time emptying

..........................................................................................

Even in the gardens, the ripped sky

of jets passing—

Even in the way the spruces balk
                    as if they could touch them—voice saying

            *not mine*     even in water

.........................................................................................

pulled by the edges of a rock in the river     *pulled from*

...........................................................................................

Back into vortices at work below the surface

oil-stained pocket of gravity

only perceivable by

convoy of its own swirling          *enormous brown leaves*

going over the falls          *can't just walk away from—*

helpless pink flowers and attendant bees     can't stop

sudden electric trees

Big-toothed maple

discharging

# Thanksgiving

I was happy, paradise

was a physical thing

*Rhus*

typhina dissecta

cutleaf

*Rhus*

typhina staghorn

sumac

. . . . . . . . . . . . . . . . . . . . . . . . . . . . . . . . . . . . . . . . . . . . . . . . . . . . . . . . . . . . . . . . . . . . . . . . . . . . . . . . . . . . . .

If I were dressed like

the sun

*red-edge*

*gold-edge*

Rhus typhina

ground brown
and holy

edge

unscorched by tiller

Overwhelmed by the sight of          —at dinner

big-toothed maple
          and cello

    Big-toothed maple
          and western prairie smoke

*Hello*

..........................................................................................................

The girl and the world that does this to me—

    Abandoned weediness

        moved back into prairie—errant—weediness

        wind in my mouth

   everything starts to wild up

.............................................................................................................

The girl and the world—*mud salt crystals rocks water*

helpless going over

the falls—overcome

by the feeling

if two people are kissing

they are doing it right

...................................................................................

four chords

and blankets

four chords

and night

holiness or

numbness

holiness four chords or blankness

## Here to Spread Light On

The lights turn the ceiling on

into goldleaf—all of them, makes me

a messenger—*each*

*of these trees is amazing.* I see

branches arc lightning, Lionel Messi on TV

and am convinced he will always be perfect—that bravery is

a girl in the park who could not look brighter. I ignore

only so much as I can handle—no such thing

as *more* perfect. We don't fall in love

just to cling—we open

all the windows. I had wanted to show you

before—a new lane of music

and walking off into the kitchen after. The sun

is fast laughter—long enough

to watch the windows change

into lingering street bells—*meant*

*never to die*—map only and archive

Arcady, the future, etc.—brighter than

our mistakes. Like Prospero said

no harm done. No drowning mark

upon my soul. Bicycles just

heavens I hadn't seen—a whole

new planet orbiting. Literally

under orchids

moving in the moonlight—that noise

small white petals in the street—one star

                    orchard

# Sounds (Second Walk)

Slow example falling from cedars—

snow caught in a streetlight, *like it was breathing*—
sudden chill in the line

in *Sounds* this morning—

*To be the mast of*
*such great admiral*

...................................................................................

and moved

out into the street

I watch the clumsy

grace of bicyclists in January

unblushing the sky, shamed of nothing

suddenly my life

makes sense: I get along

until the cloud just collapses—

I am standing on the freeway

and cars move by like drunk panthers

I am loved again

like there was future again—

*in street clothes*

*take small notes*

*unfolding*

*chorus.* I can't just

go out and buy a wheat-colored soul—an overgrown

path in the weeds behind the school

rough elm edges

affection        rattled like a furnace

behind French doors—

Red

orange-red

yellow-red green—

I had wanted to be

a courtyard full of street lights

No cars, just    the sidewalk when it rains—

makeshift forests

where there weren't any

yesterday—the kind of line

that lets you out into the world, the glimpses

you get when the wall shifts

to windows enough

for lights, Christmas

to stream by. I want to be

the picture of myself going out—

the sidewalk when it rains. These sayings

calm me down. Rooftop tennis courts

Ice-crystals, halo

reddish inner edge—

Sun-stormy aurora—*aurora at speeds*

## Dear Beings I Can Feel Your Hands

*Small voice of my father saying*
            *little piece of dirt facing*
      *small boat harbor—*

On Tuesday, meteor

and then on

Thursday, riptides. Spouting

Horn—What *am* I? To be

the mast of such great admiral—

Sit down. Dear beings, I am afraid

I have lost my ruthlessness and cunning

along with a bay horse and turtledove. There

are flowers stuck to the ceiling. Seriously.

What have I near the water? My family

moves around me. I have decided

nothing (*scares* me). I look out across the water

and a spindly black spider

turns out to be a tide crab. Little sister

saying *that's a moth's wing*—up close

Set waves, tide

more like a feeling—my mother saying          *look*

*at how many people died while we were away—*

Thin series of blurs

like I was never there at all

Like the other day I heard a woman

talking to her friend at the bar   *I feel*

*like I'm not good enough. I'll never make money*

*again, never fall in love. I don't know*

*where to go when the doors close—*

I can't just go out and buy a wheat-colored soul

write a sadder poem—startled

by windows curved up in the shape of

fins. Up and behind my head

the shadows on the table spin

for us. We are in love—if I could

spend my life    beneath palm fronds

into which walk          little birds and saunterers

Clouds wrapped around iceplants       if I could only

find *one* of the letters to God

in the street—I am still new to town

The kids on the lawn go around

the light. I don't get it. The first word

I hear on my birthday

is *windowbox*—charming of treetops

and songs on the radio

calm me down. Disarmed

but hopeful—*thank you*

I look up and

*cathedral,*
        *spotlight*

not having to

        imagine beautiful rooftops

—I find myself in that

§

And the feeling of girls laughing downstairs—

lucky enough just to scan the flights of birds

stand under bleachers      in the snow

blurting out kisses—like a man

the cards kept urging forward

the world so rare it ripples

in the photos I develop, I tell the clerk     *go somewhere*

and make yourself happy. All the lights in the ceiling

say *flood*. Make me happy—*feeling of.* I say

a feeling left of

windblown. I want to live

in a world where rooftop tennis courts

covered in confectioners' snow stadium lights

on all the south-facing windows—world where

gates ajar          rend my prayer

where
                    *wren—*

2

# Anglers (So Soon)

Hulking
the way it comes at me
two quivering palms full
of pine needle, the need
you say they signify, the lack
the way we wrap ourselves up against—
If I had any say in this
I'd say *rolls in laughter*
earth's last plantation of happiness
sky, rainweed, the way the bead
of dew against my face has
to *do* with anything this morning
unties me, rallies
round energies
bourn by all your tongue is
born with
all the jackals of the heart

Your tongue that sits
astride numerous
fresh with
grove significance
shot through with
what comes to you
wastrel or champion
   heart thing
those words you get out
of my mouth when
the tin of primer tips
and we *all* jump back, just like Nathan did
because in my dream it's me
the explosion become syllable
the hillside, having suddenly to do with dresses
cleft-tongue of men and angels
a hardware store, an Orange Julius
stand next to a beautiful unfurled
   *I'm sorry I love you*
Shot through with bone

It is the heart that hulks
kisses someone else
and I'm a white table in public, the way
water pours from a canticle into a glass
Alembic, I guess. The day you—
through me cold water
a front door
my friends and family
happy finally. Revelatory,
I know. Tellingly—I do. The day
you are up and delicate
I realize what you're up against—real power
criminals,   well-dressed

So talk to your grandmother, go
to the party with someone, go
to another—jumping across
pins on the ice—I used to
be the richest man in the world
so I know what's not mine
—

I know I've been gone a long time
but the future is
love or isn't future at all
—

It leaves me
watching ships disappear
in the rain, anchors dissolving
in my mouth, the overwhelming kind
of gratitude, saying hello to a lost friend
in and after the birds' noise, a star
so bright so red I think of the light
the way its job is already done
when it gets to us. What
family, what
gets us

## Midnight Suns

No work anymore
in the glacier troughs
majestic stutter, tiny
bottle of Icelandic
vodka, and further
more impressed by
the originality of arctic foxes
real bravery, ice sheets—
don't know what to do with
      myself having never felt more
lost and found you
and a door—let go, fall
for something else, to which
of the following
do you say yes? All
foreign movies, ice blond
and blue—the trees
aren't worried
about you, they're
trying to tell you
even in the gardens
      *we get the idea*

for fireworks

      from flowers

any aster, if it opens

      says something

beautiful, probably

      about a peony—*I was waiting*

I was waiting

      for you

to come

         to your senses

## As the Sky Contained My Garden, I Opened My Door

If anything

      of the moment persists—

helpless, this grace

      that collects

at the edges—I *want* you

      and get free drinks instead,

open shirts, all from our old friends—

      I can't tell you how much

kindness means just then

      what the look given is worth

and as such how disappointing

      selfishness—how we survive

our own sleep is a question

      but not tenderness

I see it in the hands of a waitress

      an always almost

shining thing—it's ok

      if you want to

let go, to meld

      welcome me

home again

# The Disaster Takes Care of Everything

There is somewhere
the perfect you in a room
with no boundaries and full
of light—the torch
of chin, hips, thighs, throat
light—my hands
start shaking
smell like flowers
hours after the disaster
all resonant harmonics—traffic
padding down the shoreline tanks
on the beach still in my body
far from any collection of falling
for example airplanes or my—
              I kept quiet mostly
except when I didn't, shuffled
the self around, measured faults in the ark
looked for correspondence
      what it means

carrying carry

      tender mercy, looking

down at you through

           the trees again

again saying *don't devolve*

     *into a lesser you*

         don't be base—

## Adumbrations

Otherwise, everything was aces
furniture of future says
            *oncoming, stutter*
that you are beautiful
have always been so
don't have to
listen to anyone. Listen
I like you, every time
you think, *as in the other spring—*
amazed by the shockwave
one huge cricket makes
in my ears and elsewhere, clockwise—
how do you know when
someone is looking at you?
That electrician in your neck
30 and bleeding
—don't want to be that
money kind of confidence
a healthy fear of
the messenger. Underdog
some arena of
song, pushed through the radio
*I need you I don't need you*
anymore

## Page of Swords

So take care of yourself, learn how
to take better pictures, breathe
into your hips, braver please
give love credit for
the way I live
that *call me*
kind of feeling
frenzied, lupine
the card I draw
blushing in your breast
pocket undressing
freedom I know you
know you understand

## Hymnal Oranges

Buoyed by a ukelele
my friends' beautiful
faces on TV
—
Because as soon as we can read
our own nakedness, eden is foreign
to us—exegesis always already
baggage, the question of how
how we see changes
everything, oranges
for instance, the inscrutable meaning
of *this* Mardi Gras—Danielle sighs
not for the reasons
you might think—a day that means
at least two things
from here on out—a line from Outside
that might not sound like the eternal
verse it was to us when
right then—*for it was for God so*
loved and disabused
not to perish, any whosoever
learns to say it
sing songs

## Masada

We are all going to the same restaurant, we all forget our names, and the wind
will never be the same again—*so, yes: joy*
—
I repeat that I am not frightened
        turn my head back up
toward the last horizon, the letters
under the sky all hidden
meanings float down here to us
and our little wine-bottle lives explode—the light
between power lines, picture where
I was or would have been
thirteen years on the side of a mountain
or rather ramp there
conveyor—so sad
to see it all built by the hands
of our loved ones and occasions
done—all the days I don't have
memories are best
so tell me I'm not familiar
any other part of now
and it's been here all along
this feeling, a lighthouse moved beyond me
of whom I am not fully keeper. I'm outside, ready to be
lion if you be wizard

# Rings

That voice inside
saying *universe*
*from a big bag of marbles*
is unsatisfying, so
we begin to wonder rightly
why the rings remain
such mystery, what that impossibly
huge hexagon over
the South Pole means
and why we are nevertheless here
And in this sense the world
isn't leper, isn't makeup, isn't joke—here too
even when we can't see it
we know we feel something
skeleton underneath
more than overwhelming
casual whiteness
form or figure below here—when
we realize the canyons weren't cut
by water in outer space, we sense
a hand pinning jacket
to our mannequin
eyes, contouring so
softly even if we can't
apprehend the body
in fabric we see infinitely

small vocabularies, each ring
of a piece, *almost*
*not there*, shining
evidence, event of this

## Door Out. Out

Feeling on the mend
Moving toward Shangri-La
I guess. I'll keep you
posted
—
Dear Cold,
Out. Out
I wake to the sound
of cars in my chest
Out. My throat, out. My nose
Out so that nothing that is not
Green can go out. Green out
and Green in—the trees outside my friend Kathryn
has said so many perfect things
I hardly know where to begin
some about her nose
some about heaven
The milky way paints a giant S in the sky

## Door Horizonal

A magic house
        *through which passes*
breaching flowers    right
where no one saw them
all new hours
full of passing and the birds here
are to be believed
—
*Here*
the birds say
everything
    *winter trees*
        *if any o-cean*

## Door the Heart

Big guns again: no speakee
indeed. Moonmoth
and grasshopper still escape our page
while distraction, with its big black dog
the horizon begs—
Because we are upstarts
we are heaven. Because we pass with wings
in the hand. Moonstruck and grass-led
I dreamt all men dropped something
a little like their heart
every day O their passing
sang

## Do o'er

That howler monkey
is mad at the world. The whole entire
thing. This I do not believe. At Har Megiddo
there were only singing strings
among the date palms. At the end of the world
there is simply quorum
      of beasts
followed by bees
      by a line that
at this
      beginning

## Caravan Door

Because someone said
I like it best when
poetry or a girl stands
on the shore
arranging fire
in the corner
of my eye
—

A garden, a room full of bells
and voices. A way out
through trees I hadn't seen—
In the night wingless creatures take flight. Do you
hear me? In the night there are frogs
jumping through
all of our windows

# Entropical (the Bulk)

Out-stubborned
emotional sea-urchin
in the shallows (stabbed me) in the shallows of the heart—
I'm the only one without a camera
which makes for difficulties, and the sun
you can't even look at it
even as it sets. I no longer have the right
to ask you who
does that look like? Do
these messages get through?
I know. I wanted to
tell you, right now
my dad is dancing funny
in front of everybody
by the iceplants
just so perfect so
I go out to the water
at the wrong time
don't talk for hours
think through it—only one answer
break up, diffuse
carelessly unto
this wave that floats
the bulk, the wastage
left with

I, this hole in my chest, left
with weekends
emotional
fur traps, no good
          reasons
a test, the affections
a thin freezing
twig of a man, someone saying almost
comically handsome, good
so long as I keep moving, so long
as my feet don't hit the ground

          *oat grass*

     *globe flower*

          *bamboo world*

     *balsa wood*

If I miss you like crazy still
not going to let it beat me. There
is someone calling my name
from the back of a restaurant
like woken from a spell, I should be
clear this is a love poem

3

# Available

My heart's ukelele you
wake me up in the morning
turn hurt to tender
opening of empty
apartment cities in China
publish the body's instructions
light giant lives on fire
strange animal
calamity, fall in love
with the ground thaw, inopportune
sticking of the tongue, the chest, all
silent with someone else living, all
our arms out here hanging
gravity on tree branches, our hands
hanging around

     —does that
make me a fool? I want to be
copper tiling on top
of the oldest buildings
a sign that reads *love*
*read it*—a crane I like twisting
in the air I like people
which makes for difficulties

Touch, boat, deep striped camisole
when I read Williams
at the bar, I almost can't stand
up—tenderness at the elbows
pork belly tacos, flickering sweaters
rattled birch branches, bracelet
skin, the shape of a body in
heat steam, thin kissed by sun—ok
I give in. All undone

## Radio Silence

Each part explosions
perhaps—for years
I coast on my tongue
let it do the walking
for both of us—unutterable
flutter in the eyes
uncross my lips and find
outside correspondence
of radiance    I lost track
of rebellion    an overturned
     begonia     so unsure
if I will ever have a voice
        again
or not miss you
black hole crane
in my nest
just like that
it's snowing again
and April all now
I feel ensconced somehow
inside treetops
like something in the air was
different about me—a differently
stirring from before. I start looking
forward to an open door
the thing that happens
next—the world
opens up, for the first time
I say *hips* and mean it

# The Hum

      Derail me
with chemistry and tinsel
I can't just go away
and quit, sort of
give up on it, my heart
if I could only find
one of the letters to—O
by now you get the picture
left and gave up
music after, the towels
in my apartment, our strata
self-inflating
baggage
      —fuck it
I take a nap with all the windows
open in a storm
*I want you to know*
can't compare
so why do it
black-out lettering
wedding pavement
enough already

# Neighborhood—18th

            —but really
spent the whole year walking
away and to
be honest
thought of Paris

*Only that it should be beautiful,*
*Only that it should be beautiful,*

—

O, beautiful

bird in the morning

make of spring a treasure

hunt of men or angels

red blue green and wet

predicament—lips, precinct

velvet, this perfect life

of glass in buildings

head-over with you

as it is, I am atwist

in the flood. A white wrist

moves past us in the courtyard

laughing—all my dreams

come back to me

true, with looks, little rivers

rolling down the rain

is so generous

I can't even say it

# Bon Vivant

The world didn't end but
the town of my friend's first love
washed away all the same—     O vanity
I lost everything, ended up
in France with diamonds
which are all that remain
—

I had ideas about water once
       they were the first
to wash away
with the rain. Through the horsehair
the world calls out its name
perfectly through open country aspen     *I am loved again*
Like future again—if I ever forget
air-conditioning has its own bigness too
the way every morning is to us
a new kind of eternal heirloom
       stars made into bedroom
laughter. The first day after apocalypse
is always solstice—proof of a kind
         of triumph
on the horizon, on the other edge of town, strung out
together like hedge limits in August, audacious, our backs to the sun
looking down the path for a mountain
we swear can't be there just
never was before

# Listening Choir

Sapling between cinder
  moths, black hole swans—the line on
      chimney stalk
 reading *love*
    *read it*—laundry steam
  cross-cut into brown
   relief—unheard of
  listening, being

   wrong, begun

  again with the need now

   not to go back

 for anyone—so forwardly

   in the courtyard

 movement, spirit

   instrument affixed to tomorrow

 by instant, maypole, the ocean

   beautiful but dumb—ok

 with that, moved away from

   ownership, sick with the noise of it

 of not what moves us

   *thank God*

 *to be casual*

   not go

 back for—

## Tranquillityite

A real new thing opening

to say just how important

a hair's breadth might be

all our unknowing

amassed near the sea, too delicate to live on the surface

so many things running over us

I think I cry as I perceive

blood in the minerals because

breakdowns are sort of like this, I go underground

or to the moon, and everything that touches you

        shatters me. Basalt

turns out to be home for what I mean. Crystalline. Whosoever

says some rock knows what I see. Dear poetry

falling down on its face from above, thank you, thank you shouldn't

have known it was enough—O good magic

and all my new scars, I promise never to regret

        ruining my shoes

     dancing in the barn

## Botanica

Cue evening—flashbulb
of a crowd as they pass by
my window, bicycle
noise cross-hatching
the night sky—the space between
two enormous orange trees
bursting if you just give me
one glimpse of
small houses
       *each of which*
in accordance
each already chorus

*Morning kick morning, swallow morning*—just like Nathan
said. Morning twist morning into a basket, a branch set, a quiet green car—
Morning punch me in the stomach *look*
*again*

Moved toward a clearing
for the first time this autumn
this evening and a picnic basket
unloading itself with both hands—
      A horizon
small hands of a child and
reaching forward
picking fruit
the thin sound of a train whistle
moves through the living room

Walking downtown today
I saw the most perfect rooftops
*The need to go outside now*
with a brown oilcloth
jacket and register the time
signature of my street after it rains
—

Morning walk morning downtown today
Morning walk morning home
through the cranes—I had wanted
to be a shard of broken light
on the windowsill—brass bands
behind every tree branch
sheer torn strips of
yellow light before
first autumn wilderness
a small group of houses
near the gate
each of which
its own concordance
each breaking forward

## Last Pier

There is a world in the world
in which we are perfect, every light
comes not from the ceiling but
beyond and we are worth it—I stare at the eyelash
on my lens and listen to Jens Lekman, trying
to make a wish      *and the sun rose over the city*—
about warmth. Minutes before I leave
I realize what's already done. Through
the yawning of straw, how could you
be more beautiful? You can
hear new music on the streets of Tel Aviv
if you want to. Exactly
a revelation and so much more
welcome company. And then
I'm all      *mint leaves, white brick, steadfast*
*sun, laughter in the trees*
          *oh my baby*—To me
the stones in the street and steps
of people passing stand lovely
as monuments to nothing. And a woman
at the table next to me asks
                    *what is this*
*"conspirator heart?"* An animal midair
between sheets. A world
in which I have made mistakes
and we are still perfect—I call it every night
and the song "Cherokee," *kissing me*
all better all right done already

# Every Blessed Thing Is Elusive

And proven by the bluest bird
ever to alight, my teacher
singing unangered by
an olive tree
   unanchored
no auger for the ground
but sky
—

Unendangered at sunrise
the greenery is leaving filled
with seagulls and miles
of evening speak—ago. Ago. It's true
a short fantasia is best, beautiful cava comes
& I sit by the fan in Reviva and Celia's
O tumbleweed, with your fool hair
and good clean desert
I could comb nothing out of it. Nothing
that isn't already spun and rowed
and also sun. What plane
descending? What clouds keeping
pace? There is more
to shadows on the fanblades
than anything I have to say, so: Ago
Ago. The first time I understand
the word is in dreams—the first time in weeks
my face isn't broken by something outside
breaking me. Imagine
shapes slipping across a shadow, like shirts
thrown over your head—amen. I give
in. Thin tall and American
none of the streets here look the same

# Sedes (for Hanna)

String lights        strewn across

          the underside of a still glass white

     wedding tent—*that this*

    *isn't easy for me*    doesn't mean it isn't easy—a seat from which
to enter the world—thin rows of desert

                    flowers not giving up

          red dirt stalks

             all grown up

to light. They don't know how to go backwards

               why even try—

.................................................................................

     As much as you wish

    we could be
    a seat from which
    with all the bravery
    of Ely or Levi, or any
    other angels of this
    clear lilynight sky
    we can be—I *know*
    how much Hanna and the sea
    changed me. The truth is green
    things never really die—I calm down
    at the sight—I don't
    understand protest songs
    in the street but know sky blue wool
    with my grandmother is beautiful
    in Israel—and I let go, open up to
    tantivy on rooftops, awake

as my name might mean, bent
down branch under tender
everything, so relax—
We go over the cliffs at last

## Blackout

Night over asphalt—passages in the snow—night over asphalt—
just wanted to be a host—a place for brightness to pass over
a million different animals all crashing into a kitchen and break-
ing nothing—keep thinking: *God moves to the ends of our prepositions*
like an open shirt—suddenly it's all leaky doors and thunder-
storms like forgetting something—it's all green—and then a
blackout everyone in streets

§

the wind that hit

those grasses

was an animal. I mean you

can see it

but only in patches. Only

by the yellow light

its teeth flashes off

I was driving downtown

when what I thought

was chandeliers

     was sky actually

teethed on two sides

     by exposure to buildings and trees

a new kind of world—*I believe you*

     and it really is glorious—really

something else

     Not the real but stuck to it—

Not full, *shot through with*

     *light*—if I ever stop thinking

this is a wilderness

     pepsi can forest

in the tall rusty bushes

     growing through steel dark

bleachers, echo of

     somebody else's for-rent

whisper on the phone—if I ever

wanted to be this carousel

of night sounds—all I can think of

is I want to be an extra pair

of movie-set lights

I was standing in flowers

inverted by bell shapes

and suddenly everything's done

so forwardly—

## Found Well

Not forgotten just not there
white flowers
in a column, sea shaped air
receding every morning
I stare, saying I am sure
something will happen

I want to be in love and all
the birds keep laughing
opening, opening
Levi I think the heart doesn't skip
but leaps, sends off between
limbs its dream and fingers
crossed helplessly

And what do I want? Music
moved beyond me—cradle
and smell of a new home
from the one I've known
a brand new nursery
I've never seen
sawgrass, meant more
than I do right now
when I'm not looking
and my beer foams over
as I call your name. I gently blow
over the corona. All the white
laughter happens. All flowers

ACKNOWLEDGMENTS

"Thanksgiving" references Robert Smithson's *Spiral Jetty*.

"Sounds (Second Walk)" includes text from Thoreau's chapter "Sounds" in *Walden*.

"Dear Beings I Can Feel Your Hands" draws its title from a line in Robin Blaser's "Image Nation 5," from *The Holy Forest: Collected Poems of Robin Blaser*, rev. and expanded ed., ed. Miriam Nichols (Berkeley: University of California Press, 2006), 149. Used by permission of the University of California Press and the Estate of Robin Blaser.

"As the Sky Contained My Garden, I Opened My Door" takes its title from a line in "Transcription of Organ Music" in *Collected Poems, 1947–1980*, by Allen Ginsberg. © Allen Ginsberg; used by permission of HarperCollins. It is also indebted to *Paterson* and William Carlos Williams.

"The Disaster Takes Care of Everything" draws its title from Maurice Blanchot's *Writing the Disaster*.

"Every Blessed Thing Is Elusive" takes its title from a line by Donald Revell. Donald Revell, excerpt from "Given Days" from *My Mojave*. Copyright © 2003 by Donald Revell. Reprinted with the permission of The Permissions Company, Inc., on behalf of Alice James Books, www.alicejamesbooks .org.

Earlier versions of some of the poems in this collection appeared in the following: *Jubilat, Colorado Review, the tiny, Bat City Review, H_NGM_N, Word for/ Word, Rhino, Iron Horse Review, Phoebe, Painted Bride Quarterly,* and *Manor House Quarterly.*

Special thanks to Hanna for her patience, love, and support; Nathan and Brenda for their friendship and guidance; Geoff and Kathryn for their family; Don and Claudia for their home and teaching; Levi, Derek, Eli, Kirsten, Stacy, Christine, Chris, Sam, Brian, Carl, Laird, Selah, Eleni, Bin, and the University of Denver for constituting a community of such good humor, direction, and faith. And finally thanks to my family, without whom none of this would be possible. I remain eternally grateful.